ATTACK IN IRAQ

By Christopher Schafer

Visit us at www.abdopub.com

Published by ABDO & Daughters, an imprint of ABDO Publishing Company, 4940 Viking Drive, Suite 622, Edina, Minnesota 55435.

Printed in the United States.

Edited by: Cory Gunderson
Contributing Editors: Sheila Rivera, Paul Joseph
Graphic Design: Arturo Leyva, David Bullen
Cover Design: Castaneda Dunham, Inc.
Photos: AP/Wide World, Corbis
Source: Star Tribune, pages 32 and 33

Library of Congress Cataloging-in-Publication Data

Schafer, Christopher.
Attack in Iraq / Christopher Schafer.
p. cm.--(War in Iraq)
Includes bibliographical references and index.
Summary: Describes the events that led up to the United States attacking Iraq, as well as the war itself and some of the immediate aftermath.
ISBN 1-59197-493-3
1. Iraq War, 2003--Juvenile literature. [1. Iraq War, 2003.] I. Title. II. Series.

DS79.76 .S328 2003
956.7044'3--dc21

2003052304

Table of Contents

Al-Qaeda terrorists crashed two planes into the World Trade Center, in New York City, on September 11, 2001.

PREPARING FOR WAR

On September 11, 2001, terrorists hijacked four commercial airplanes. Two planes slammed into the twin towers of New York City's World Trade Center. Another hit the Pentagon in Washington, D.C. The fourth plane crashed in a field in Pennsylvania. These were the worst terrorist attacks ever on U.S. soil.

After the attacks, the U.S. government declared a War on Terrorism and began searching for those responsible. They determined that the September 11 attacks were conducted by the terrorist group al-Qaeda. U.S. intelligence knew that many al-Qaeda members were hiding in Afghanistan. But the Taliban ruled Afghanistan. It refused to turn the terrorists over to U.S. officials. The United States promised to use military force if needed to apprehend terrorists involved in the September 11 attacks. Still the Taliban would not cooperate.

The U.S. military went to war in Afghanistan and destroyed the Taliban. It also captured several al-Qaeda terrorists who were hiding in the nation's mountains. Since then, the U.S. government has worked to catch terrorists all over the world, to ensure the safety of the American people.

To this end, the United States implemented a new national defense strategy. Under the new policy, the U.S. government would not wait to be attacked first. It would take preemptive military action against nations considered to be threats to national security.

To implement the new policy, U.S. government and intelligence officials needed to identify countries that posed a threat. President George W. Bush named Iraq as one of these nations. In his State of the Union address on January 29, 2002, Bush said Iran, Iraq, and North Korea were an "axis of evil."

The U.S. government believed that Iraq's government had weapons of mass destruction, and supported terrorist groups such as al-Qaeda. U.S. secretary of state Colin Powell labeled Iraq as one of seven countries that supported terrorism. Secretary Powell based this decision on information that linked Iraq to terrorism.

For example, in 1993, the Iraqi Intelligence Service attempted to assassinate former U.S. president George H.W. Bush and Kuwaiti leader, Jabir al-Ahmad al-Jabir al-Sabah, with a car bomb in Kuwait. Kuwaiti officials learned of the plan, stopped the attempt, and arrested 16 people.

In Iraq, terrorist groups found safe harbor and carried out attacks that resulted in the deaths of many other people. Iraq provided a home for the Palestine Liberation Front. This group staged air attacks against Israel. Its leader, Abu Abbas, was involved in hijacking the cruise ship *Achille Lauro* in 1985. During the hijacking, American Leon Klinghoffer was murdered.

Iraqi soldiers dressed as suicide bombers and carrying mock explosives participate in a military parade.

The Mujahedin-e-Khalq Organization also operated inside Iraq. This group was responsible for terrorist acts against Iran. It was also involved in the murders of several U.S. citizens, both military and civilian.

The Abu Nidal Organization also operated from inside Iraq's borders. The group is responsible for terrorist attacks in 20 countries. Its members have killed or wounded nearly 900 people.

Secretary Powell also noted that Iraqi president Saddam Hussein supported terrorism by giving $10,000 to the families of Palestinian suicide bombers. Families received this money as a reward for the bombers' actions. In April 2002, Saddam increased the reward to $25,000.

This information, along with other classified intelligence, convinced the U.S. government that Saddam must be removed from power. But President Bush knew Saddam might not be removed by diplomatic means. It was possible that military force would be needed. To secure the authority to use military force, Bush needed the approval of the U.S. Congress.

On October 10, 2002, the House of Representatives voted 296-133 in support of the president. The next day, the Senate gave its approval with a 77-23 vote. The bill was supported by almost all of the Republicans. Influential Democrats such as Tom Daschle and Dick Gebhardt also supported the bill, demonstrating the bipartisan support that the president had in Congress on this important measure.

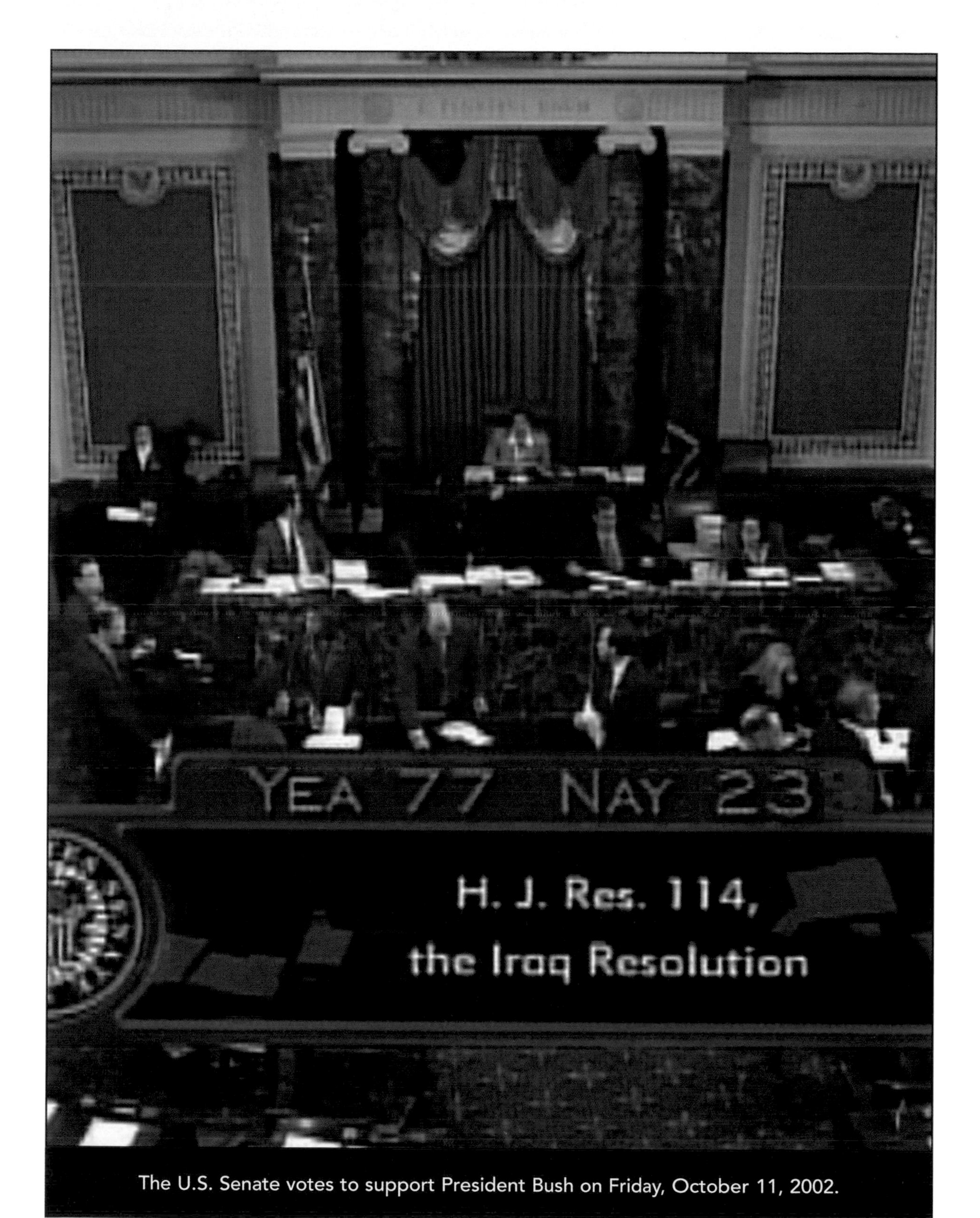

The U.S. Senate votes to support President Bush on Friday, October 11, 2002.

Backed by the congressional bill that approved military force, President Bush turned to the problem of removing Saddam from power. This posed a difficult situation. Saddam had been ignoring world leaders and international law for years.

The U.S. government knew that the Iraqi government had defied international law and used chemical weapons. Most of these attacks were launched during the Iran-Iraq War. But Iraq had also used poison gas against the Kurds who lived in the mountains of northern Iraq. In total, experts estimate that Iraqi poison gas attacks killed or wounded more than 20,000 people.

The world's nations wanted to stop Saddam's use of weapons of mass destruction. When the Persian Gulf War ended in 1991, Iraq agreed to many United Nations (UN) rules. The country accepted an agreement to end its weapons of mass destruction programs. It was also banned from possessing other weapons, such as long-range missiles. The UN sent a team of weapons inspectors into Iraq to look for prohibited weapons. The inspectors needed to confirm that Iraq had destroyed the weapons it had, and that no more were in production.

But the inspections did not go smoothly. Iraq's government would not cooperate with the inspectors. Saddam believed the UN team had too many British and American members. Iraqi government officials distrusted the British and the Americans. They thought these people might be spies. The inspection team left Iraq on October 31, 1998. Team members said the Iraqi government refused to allow inspections of many sites, including some residential buildings.

Some world governments believed Saddam still had weapons of mass destruction. And with Iraq's ties to terrorism and terrorist organizations, they were afraid that Saddam's regime might use these weapons against other nations, or give these weapons to terrorist groups.

On November 8, 2002, the UN passed Resolution 1441. It said Iraq would have to disarm all weapons of mass destruction, and allow weapons inspectors back into the country to look anywhere they wanted. If Iraq did not comply with the resolution, it would face serious consequences.

Iraq's government initially rejected the proposal on November 12, 2002. Yet, one day later the Iraqi government reversed its decision and accepted the resolution. On November 18, UN inspectors went back into Iraq.

U.S. government officials questioned the usefulness of the inspections. They didn't believe that the weapons inspections were effective. They believed the Iraqis were deceiving UN inspectors. They also thought Iraqis were lying to the inspectors and hiding banned weapons.

The United States declared Iraq in breach of UN Resolution 1441. President Bush began to exercise the authority bestowed by Congress in October. He ordered soldiers into the Middle East to prepare for war.

Meanwhile, the U.S. government asked the UN to enforce Resolution 1441. The resolution had said Iraq would face serious consequences if it did not comply. U.S. officials believed Iraq was not in compliance. Secretary Powell appealed to the UN to enforce its resolution. President Bush and British prime minister Tony Blair prepared to introduce a new resolution that would allow military force to bring Iraq into compliance.

But other nations did not agree with the United States. Many believed that Iraq did not have any banned weapons. They thought weapons inspectors just needed more time to prove this. They wanted to continue to explore diplomatic processes to continue inspections. In the UN, Russia, China, Germany, and France stood against the United States and the United Kingdom. So Bush and Blair decided against a new resolution.

On March 17, 2003, President Bush issued a warning to Saddam Hussein. Bush said, "Saddam Hussein and his sons must leave Iraq within 48 hours. Their refusal to do so will result in military conflict commenced at a time of our choosing."

By this time, the United States and its allies had 297,000 soldiers in the Middle East. They also had heavy armor that included 700 helicopters, 1,600 tanks, and 5 aircraft carrier groups. Small groups of U.S. Special Forces were at work in northern Iraq organizing Kurdish opposition groups. The U.S. National Guard also called up thousands of reservists. Coalition soldiers gathered along the border between Iraq and Kuwait. They waited for Saddam to make a decision. The dictator refused to leave Iraq.

U.S. Marines take up positions in the Kuwaiti desert for a possible war with Iraq.

THE FIRST STRIKE

Saddam's 48 hours ran out at 8 P.M. eastern standard time on March 19, 2003. An hour and a half later, true to his word, President Bush authorized the use of military force in Iraq. A White House representative called Prime Minister Blair to let him know that the attack had begun.

The United States did not fight alone. While it was the largest nation involved in the conflict, it was part of a group of nations that were also committed to destroying Iraq's weapons of mass destruction and removing Saddam from power. This group of allies formed the Coalition of the Willing.

Every coalition member contributed to the war effort. Some countries, such as Australia and the United Kingdom, offered full military support. Japan promised to donate money to help rebuild Iraq after the war. Romania said the United States could set up military bases in its country. Poland offered to send 200 troops. The Czech Republic said it would send a chemical-biological unit to help in case such weapons were used against coalition soldiers.

Many observers thought the war would be a massive campaign. Some thought the U.S. military would use all of its weapons to quickly defeat and disarm Iraq. U.S. military officials wanted to defeat Iraq quickly, but they did not want Iraqi civilians to be killed. To minimize the possibility of civilian casualties, the military called for precise attacks on "targets of opportunity."

U.S. military officials identified one such target just before the war began. They believed that Saddam, his sons Uday and Qusay, and several Iraqi military officials were in a compound in southern Baghdad. The compound had two buildings and a separate underground bunker. The U.S. military believed that Saddam and his top aides were in the bunker, and would be for a few hours. Central Intelligence Agency (CIA) director George Tenet told Bush that this compound was "one really ripe" target. The U.S. government modified its existing war plan to include an attack on the compound.

COALITION OF THE WILLING

Afghanistan
Albania
Angola
Australia
Azerbaijan
Bulgaria
Colombia
Costa Rica
The Czech Republic
Denmark
Dominican Republic
El Salvador
Eritrea
Estonia
Ethiopia
Georgia
Honduras
Hungary
Iceland
Italy
Japan
Kuwait
Latvia
Lithuania
Macedonia
Marshall Islands
Micronesia
Mongolia
The Netherlands
Nicaragua
Palau
Panama
The Philippines
Poland
Portugal
Romania
Rwanda
Singapore
Slovakia
Solomon Islands
South Korea
Spain
Tonga
Turkey
Uganda
Ukraine
The United Kingdom
The United States
Uzbekistan

A Tomahawk land attack missile is fired from the deck of the USS *Bunker Hill.*

Ships stationed in the Persian Gulf and the Red Sea fired nearly 40 Tomahawk cruise missiles at Iraqi targets. The Tomahawk is the U.S. military's most-often used missile. It uses the Global Positioning System to find its target. These missiles can travel distances of up to 1,000 miles (1,609 km) at speeds of up to 550 miles per hour (885 km/h).

The attack continued, assisted by a force of F-117 Nighthawk bombers. They dropped a brand-new bomb, called the EGBU-27. This laser-guided bomb weighed 2,000 pounds (907 kg). The EGBU-27 was so accurate that it exploded within 3 feet (1 m) of its target. This accuracy was possible even when it was dropped from heights of 20,000 feet (6,096 m).

Many of these missiles and bombs were directed at the compound Saddam was believed to be in. This attack on Saddam's compound illustrated the U.S. military's decapitation strategy. This strategy required coalition forces to kill Saddam Hussein and other important Iraqi leaders. Military officials hoped that if Saddam were dead, Iraqi soldiers would surrender. This would shorten the war and reduce civilian casualties.

In addition to the decapitation strategy, military leaders worked to weaken Iraq's defenses by pounding Iraq's capital, Baghdad. Coalition forces knew it would be important to conquer this city. Baghdad was home to Iraq's leadership, and capturing it meant taking control of the country. Without Baghdad, Saddam would have no home to command his soldiers from.

At 10:15 P.M. eastern standard time on March 19, President Bush appeared on national television to inform the American people that the war had officially begun. Bush said, "American and coalition forces are in the early stages of military operations to disarm Iraq, to free its people and to defend the world from grave danger." In his national address, Bush also spoke to the men and women of the armed services. He told them, "The enemies you confront will come to know your skill and bravery. The people you liberate will witness the honorable and decent spirit of the American military."

Bush closed the speech by promising that the United States would be victorious in its war effort. Bush told the American people, "I assure you, this will not be a campaign of half measures, and we will accept no outcome but victory . . . We will bring freedom to others and we will prevail."

A few hours later, Saddam appeared on Baghdad television. He openly condemned the attacks and said America would be punished. Saddam called the attacks a "shameful crime." He said, "We promise you that Iraq, its leadership and its people will stand up to the evil invaders. They will face bitter defeat, God willing." The video made it appear as though Saddam had survived the attacks on the bunker.

People everywhere saw Saddam on television that night. Yet, American officials were not sure if the man in the video really was Saddam, because he was known to have body doubles. Saddam's body doubles had undergone plastic surgery so they would look more like him. They were trained to walk, act, and move as Saddam did. The

U.S. president George W. Bush addresses the nation on March 19, 2003.

doubles presented themselves as Saddam in order to confuse his enemies. Opponents never knew if they were seeing the real Saddam or a body double.

Experts had done much research on Saddam's body doubles. German forensic pathologist Dr. Dieter Buhmann had studied Saddam's appearance for a German public television station. Buhmann evaluated more than 450 images of Saddam and his doubles. While doing so, he took measurements of each image's face, eyebrows, and mustache. In his final report, Buhmann concluded that Saddam had three body doubles.

Jerrald Post had worked with the CIA studying Saddam. When he saw Saddam on television Post said, "My initial reaction was, 'Gee. That does not look like him.'" Investigators wondered if it was really Saddam on the video. They weren't sure if it was Saddam looking poorly, or one of his body doubles.

U.S. officials analyzed a tape of Saddam's television appearance. They compared the voice on the tape to other recordings of Saddam's voice. After the analysis, officials stated that it was in fact Saddam's voice on the tape. Yet, this still didn't mean that Saddam was alive. It was possible that Saddam Hussein had taped the television appearance before the attack. This left American officials unsure if Saddam was dead or alive.

Iraqi television shows Saddam urging the people of Baghdad to "strike the enemy with force."

IRAQ COUNTERATTACKS

Soon Iraq's military launched a counterattack. The United States had previously told the Iraqi government not to set its oil wells on fire. This would cause major environmental damage. It would also waste valuable resources that belonged to Iraq's people. But Iraqi officials did not heed the warning. To create a smoke screen they hoped would confuse coalition pilots, Iraqi forces set oil wells on fire.

Critics of the war blamed the United States for the oil fires. Many people, including the Iraqis, believed that the United States was fighting Iraq to get possession of its oil reserves. Iraqi officials believed that if it destroyed its oil wells, the United States would have less oil to take if it won the war.

Coalition forces rushed to extinguish the oil fires. During the Persian Gulf War, Iraq had set fire to more than 700 oil wells in Kuwait. The environmental damage from the burning oil was enormous. Coalition forces wanted to avoid a similar disaster from happening again.

On Thursday, March 20, 2003, Iraq continued its counterattack by firing three missiles at coalition forces. Patriot missiles intercepted the first two missiles. The third missile broke in half in midair and fell to the ground. Allied forces thought some of the missiles were Scuds.

This was one of the weapons that Iraq was forbidden to have under the UN agreement reached after the Persian Gulf War.

U.S. officials said that two of the three missiles were Scuds. But British officials said that only one was a Scud. The third missile was an al-Samoud. Coalition forces were concerned about Scud missiles. They knew that Saddam could attach chemical or biological warheads to the missiles, turning them into weapons of mass destruction.

Each time a Scud missile was launched, coalition forces were in danger. They were forced to put on gas masks and chemical protection suits. They did not know if the missiles would have chemical or biological weapons inside them. On the night of these attacks, troops had to put their suits on three times in two hours.

As the allies and the Iraqis fired missiles at one another, word of the war spread around the world. The news drew immediate reactions from both people and governments. U.S. allies commended the coalition's efforts to remove a brutal dictator from power and eliminate his weapons of mass destruction.

But many others opposed the war. China, Germany, France, and Russia continued to criticize the use of force in Iraq. Most Arab nations also condemned the attack. They could not support the invasion of an Islamic state by non-Muslims. Iran's foreign minister, Kamal Kharrazi, said the military attack was "unjustifiable and illegitimate." Soon protesters around the world gathered to voice their opposition to the war.

SHOCK AND AWE

The U.S. government officials had hoped that the first strike on Saddam and his leaders would end the war. They wanted the war to be over quickly, with as few people killed as possible.

Officials in the U.S. Department of Defense said no more attacks would come if someone other than Saddam took control of the country. They also said that this person would have to invite the U.S. military to enter Iraq peacefully. But no new leader appeared. So the United States had to believe that Saddam was still in control of Iraq. The attacks continued.

The second phase of the attack was called Shock and Awe. This strategy was outlined in *Shock and Awe: Achieving Rapid Dominance*, a book by Harlan Ullman, L.A. Edney, and James P. Wade Jr. The Shock and Awe strategy includes pounding enemy positions so powerfully that the enemy's spirit is broken, and it sees no chance of victory. The enemy then has no choice but to surrender.

The Shock and Awe campaign began on March 21, 2003. Coalition forces hit several targets in Baghdad. They also hit other Iraqi cities such as Mosul and Kirkuk. Saddam's homes and palaces were among the

Smoke rises from a presidential palace compound in Baghdad during a night of heavy air strikes by U.S. forces.

campaign's targets. Other targets were military facilities and Baath party buildings. During the first 24 hours of the Shock and Awe campaign, coalition forces fired 1,500 bombs and Tomahawk missiles.

In the campaign, allied forces used many types of aircraft to deliver the massive firepower needed to make the Shock and Awe strategy successful. The F-14 Tomcat and F/A-18 Hornet are fighter jets, usually used to fight other planes. But in Shock and Awe, both planes were used in bombing missions. Many of these planes were launched from the aircraft carrier USS *Kitty Hawk* in the Persian Gulf.

Another important type of aircraft used during operation Shock and Awe were bombers, such as the B-52 Stratofortress, the B-1 Lancer, and the B-2 Spirit. The B-2 was the plane most often used by coalition forces. B-2 bombers use stealth technology to avoid detection by enemy radar. These powerful planes can hold nearly 40,000 pounds (18,144 kg) of weapons and ammunition. Some B-2s made a 36-hour journey to drop their bombs. They flew from Whiteman, Missouri, to conduct their missions. On the first night of the Shock and Awe campaign, B-2 bombers destroyed 92 targets in six sorties.

During the campaign, U.S. planes were able to fly into Iraq with little danger of attack. They flew under cover of night for additional protection. But the Iraqi air force was not very strong. It relied on antiaircraft guns to bring down coalition aircraft. This weak defense was no match for U.S. aviation technology.

During the Shock and Awe campaign, coalition forces hit targets everywhere in the country. The United States tried not to hurt civilians

HEROES OF THE SKY

F-14 TOMCAT

F/A-18 HORNET

B-1 LANCER

B-2 BOMBER

Allied forces used different types of aircraft to launch its massive strike on Iraq.

during these strikes. Still, some innocent civilians were killed. On March 25, 2003, Iraqi officials claimed that the number of Iraqi civilian casualties was as high as 194. At the time, the Red Cross could only confirm 14 civilian casualties. Meanwhile, various reports from Western media sources placed the Iraqi civilian death toll between 199 and 278. But no one was really certain how many civilians were accidentally killed.

A U.S. armored vehicle speeds through the desert to cross the Kuwait-Iraq border.

THE MARCH TO BAGHDAD

The ground campaign began when coalition soldiers moved across the Kuwaiti border and into southern Iraq on March 20, 2003. They also moved into Iraq from the west and the north. Allied forces slowly worked their way toward Baghdad. They faced resistance by Saddam's troops in Basra, Umm Qasr, and Najaf.

Basra is Iraq's second-largest city. It was an important coalition target because of its size. It would also be a major distribution point for humanitarian aid. British forces fought to capture Basra. By early April, they were gaining control.

Umm Qasr is a major port city on the Persian Gulf. By taking this city, the coalition could receive the food, water, and medicine being shipped to Iraq from countries all over the world. On March 22, 2003, U.S. officials declared that the struggle in Umm Qasr was "effectively over." Umm Qasr had fallen to the coalition.

Najaf, in southern Iraq, is a very important religious city for Muslims. Najaf is said to be the burial site of the prophet Muhammad's son-in-law, Ali. He is the Shiites' most important saint. U.S. forces took control of Najaf by April 2.

Even after coalition forces had secured these cities, soldiers still weren't safe. Small groups of enemy forces continued to resist. Often they shot at allied troops from the windows of nearby buildings. Sometimes they blew themselves up near allied forces, hoping to kill their enemies while killing themselves. Coalition troops had to stay alert.

Coalition forces faced other difficulties as they proceeded to Baghdad. Some of the resistance they faced came from Fedayeen Saddam and the Baath party militia. These paramilitary groups were not part of the regular Iraqi army. But they still fought against the coalition. When asked about paramilitary groups, U.S. lieutenant general William Wallace said, "The enemy we're fighting is different . . . because of paramilitary forces. We knew they were here but we did not know how they would fight."

Coalition forces quickly learned that the paramilitary forces did not fight fair. Sometimes they disguised themselves as civilians. Other times they used women and children as shields. It was also said that paramilitary groups forced Iraqi civilian men to fight in the war. If the men refused, the paramilitaries threatened to kill their families. The paramilitaries were referred to as "terrorist-like death squads."

These unconventional fighting methods made it difficult for coalition soldiers. They did not know if an approaching civilian would try to kill them or surrender. They didn't want to hurt the women and children who were forced to shield the paramilitary soldiers. Yet, despite difficult battles and sneaky enemies, the coalition focused on its main goal

of capturing Baghdad. With each victory, coalition soldiers made steady progress. This movement became known as the March to Baghdad.

Many U.S. military units were involved in the March to Baghdad. These included the First Marine Division and the army's Third Infantry Division. Another important unit was the army's 101st Airborne Division out of Fort Campbell, Kentucky.

These units traveled in convoys. Coalition forces believed that they would be safe from attack if they traveled in large numbers. They believed that the Iraqis would be less likely to attack them because they would be in numbers too great. The convoy was important in leading coalition soldiers on the March to Baghdad.

Coalition forces faced difficult opposition on their journey through Iraq to Baghdad. At the beginning of the war, experts believed Iraq had 389,000 soldiers. Eighty thousand troops were members of the Republican Guard, Saddam Hussein's best soldiers. Iraq's army was well equipped with many weapons, including 300 planes, 375 helicopters, and 5,000 tanks.

The coalition had 297,000 soldiers, 700 planes, 700 helicopters, and only 1,600 tanks in the region. So in total, Iraq's land army was much larger than the coalition forces. But despite its size, the Iraqi army was not as effective as coalition forces expected. The coalition's advanced weapons and air superiority gave it a clear advantage. In one series of battles for Baghdad's airport, coalition forces reported killing 150 Iraqis without suffering a single casualty.

COALITION TROOPS

COALITION COMBAT AIRCRAFT

COALITION HELICOPTERS

COALITION TANKS

COALITION AIRCRAFT CARRIER BATTLE GROUPS

= 30,000 soldiers

= 100 aircraft

= 100 helicopters

= 200 tanks

= 1 battle group

IRAQI TROOPS

★الله★أكبر★

IRAQI COMBAT AIRCRAFT

IRAQI HELICOPTERS

IRAQI TANKS

After battles such as these, many Iraqi soldiers chose to surrender. A massive surrender of Iraqi troops was part of the coalition's plan to end the war quickly with few casualties. To facilitate this part of the plan, months before the war began coalition aircraft dropped hundreds of thousands of leaflets on Iraq. The leaflets gave step-by-step instructions on how to surrender. By following these steps, Iraqi soldiers could demonstrate that their intention was sincere, which would reduce the risk of accidental loss of life.

In addition to the dangers presented by the Iraqi military on the March to Baghdad, coalition forces had difficulty with Iraq's climate. Strong gusts of wind blew sand across the desert, creating fierce sandstorms. One of these storms forced coalition forces to stop their movement. Helicopters had to land because they could not fly in the sand. This made it difficult for units such as the 101st Airborne's Third Brigade, which used helicopters to drop men behind enemy lines. Sandstorms meant that some units couldn't complete their missions.

WAR LEAFLETS

The Ah Fad Al Farouq Tank Bn of the 70th Arm Bde, 6th Arm Div did not comply with Coalition guidelines.

IZ D033o

Indicate you are not a threat by following these Coalition instructions:

-Park vehicles in squares, no larger than battalion size.
-Place gun barrels over back deck of vehicle.
-Stow artillery and air defense artillery systems in travel configuration.
-Display white flags on vehicles.
-No visible man portable air defense systems.
-Personnel must gather in groups, a minimum of one kilometer away from their vehicles.
-Officers may retain their sidearms, all others must disarm.
-Do not approach Coalition forces.
-Wait for further instructions.

English version

كتيبة أحفاد الفاروق التابعة للواء "٧٠" للمدرعات
في الفرقة السادسة للمدرعات لم تستجب لإرشادات الإئتلاف.

IZ D033o

أظهروا بأنكم لا تشكلون تهديدا وذلك بإتباعكم تعليمات الإئتلاف هذه

- أوقفوا آلياتكم على شكل مربعات، لا يزيد حجمها حجم الكتيبة.
- أديروا ووجهوا فواهات السبطانات نحو مؤخرة سطح الآلية.
- ثبتوا سبطانات كل قطع المدفعية ومدافع الدفاع الجوي بوضع اللارمي
- إرفعوا أعلاما بيضاء فوق آلياتكم
- تخلوا عن أجهزة الدفاع الجوي المحمولة، إتركوها بعيدة عن النظر وغير مرئية قدر الإمكان.
- على الأفراد العسكريين التجمع بشكل مجموعات على مسافة كيلومتر واحد على الأقل بعيدا عن آلياتهم
- يمكن للضباط الإحتفاظ بسلاحهم الجنبي، ولكن على الآخرين أجمعين أن يجردوا أنفسهم من السلاح.
- لا تقتربوا من قوات الإئتلاف.
- إنتظروا تعليمات إضافية.

Arabic version

CASUALTIES OF CONFLICT

As the war progressed, both sides suffered casualties. This is the saddest aspect of war, and it is also the main reason that countries avoid war if possible. The number of casualties in a war can be hard to determine. The governments of coalition countries reported all deaths. As of April 8, 2003, the coalition forces reported that 108 coalition troops had died in the war. Of the 108 soldiers who died, 53 were killed in action.

The other 55 coalition soldiers were killed in accidents. The number one cause of accidental death of coalition soldiers was helicopter crashes. Twenty-eight troops died in such accidents. Other reasons for accidental soldier deaths were drowning, vehicle accidents, and various other problems grouped as "land accidents."

Deaths on the Iraqi side were harder to count. No one was really sure how many Iraqis had died. Coalition forces knew the total number of Iraqi dead numbered in the thousands. But they didn't have an exact figure. Dana Dillon, of the research institute Heritage Foundation, said, "It's difficult to verify, especially when you're dropping bombs on people and you don't go back and count bodies."

An unidentified British soldier is evacuated due to a leg injury.

Some of the casualties were prisoners of war (POWs). POWs are soldiers who have been captured by the enemy. POWs are sometimes held until the end of the war. Sometimes their captors kill them. Sometimes, special agreements are made in which armies exchange one POW for another.

Rules for the treatment of POWs are detailed in the Geneva convention. The Geneva convention is a treaty that outlines the rules of conduct during war. It was formally adopted on August 12, 1949. The Geneva convention states that opposing armies cannot torture, execute, or harm a POW. It also states that an army is in charge of caring for all of its POWs during a war. The Geneva convention also says that the Red Cross must be able to visit any POWs.

Red Cross officials visited a coalition POW camp near Umm Qasr. The Red Cross spent several hours at the camp talking to the commander. Afterward, they toured the facility and received information about the prisoners there.

Red Cross officials were not allowed to see coalition POWs held by Iraq. Coalition forces and the Red Cross were unsure how the POWs were being treated. Coalition POWs had been interviewed on Iraqi television. Interviewing troops on television is against the Geneva convention. Coalition commanders were concerned about the safety of the POWs, but they had no way of learning about their condition.

Coalition forces were finally able to learn something about their POWs when they rescued several of them. The first rescued POW was Private Jessica Lynch. Private Lynch was a supply clerk in the 507th

Prisoners of War

Joseph Hudson

Patrick Miller

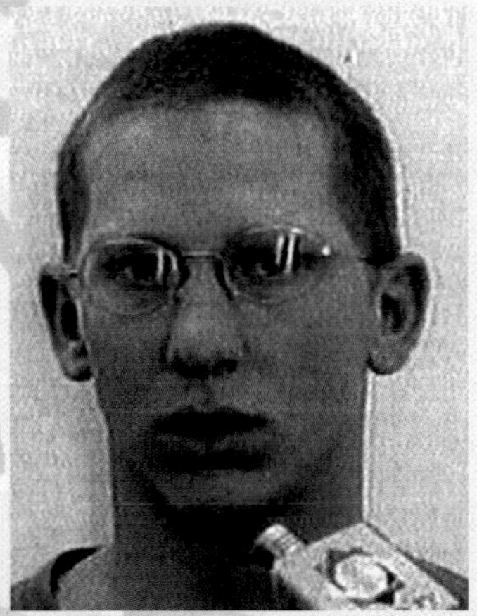

Edgar Hernandez

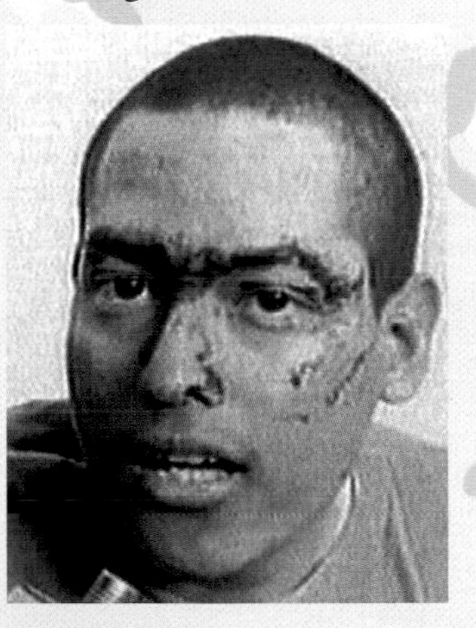

James Riley

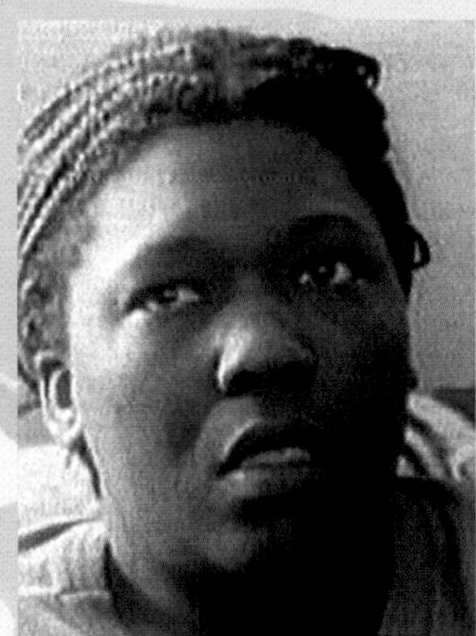

Shoshawna Johnson

These U.S. soldiers were interviewed on Iraqi television after being captured in a battle near the southern city of An Nasiriya.

Maintenance Company. She was captured when her unit became lost near An Nasiriya after making a wrong turn.

Coalition leaders did not know what had become of the 507th. Then, an Iraqi lawyer told coalition troops that he had seen an American in a hospital in An Nasiriya. A team of marines, navy SEALs, army Rangers, and air force pilots raided the hospital and rescued Private Lynch. She had injuries to her back, right arm, both legs, and her right foot and ankle. Marines also recovered the bodies of nine dead Americans from a nearby location.

Other coalition members also sustained casualties. The number of civilian losses remained unknown. It could take years to assess damage done to Iraq's environment and infrastructure. This serves as a grim reminder that even in victory, war's price is high.

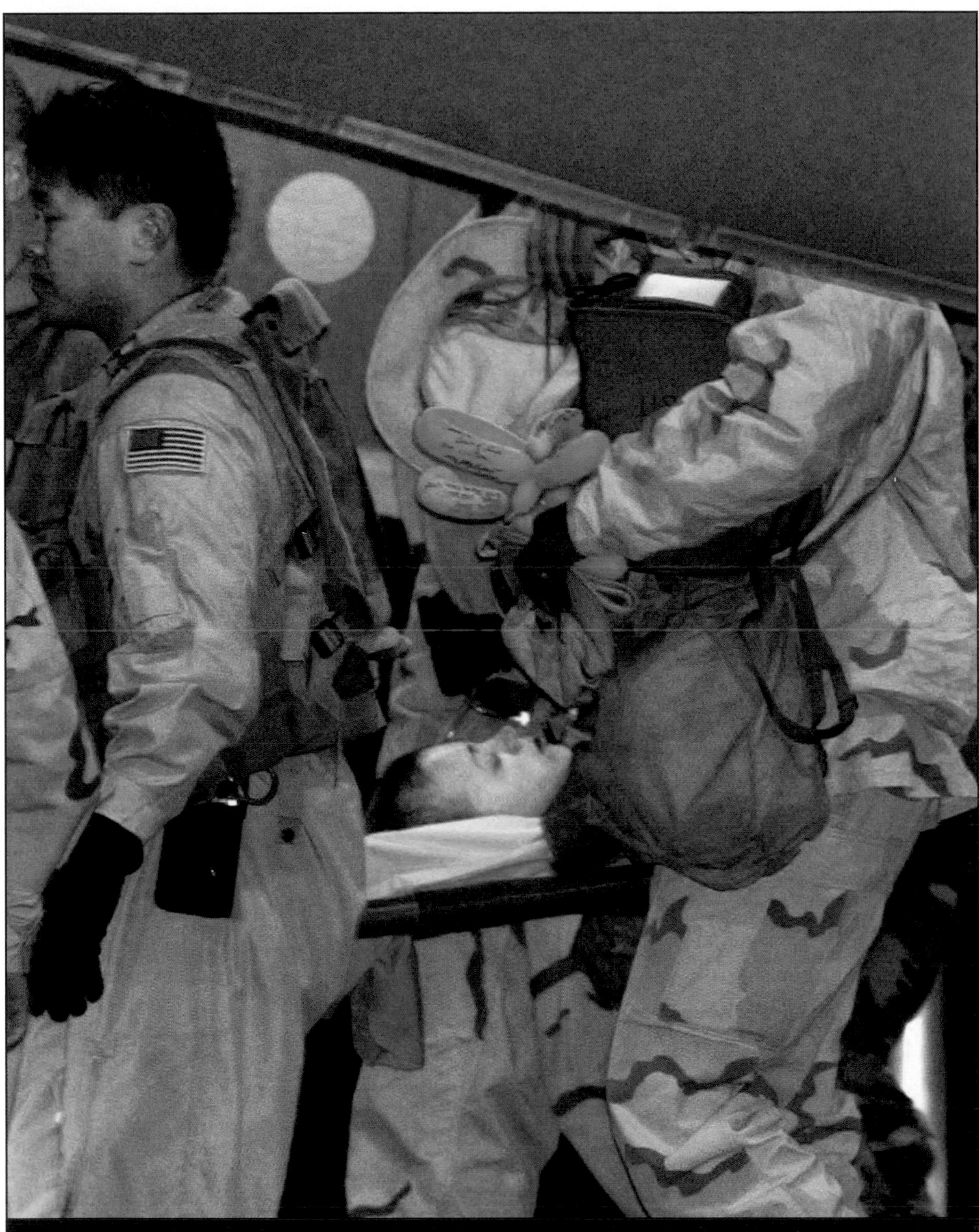

Jessica Lynch is carried on a stretcher at the U.S. air base in Ramstein, Germany. Lynch was rescued by special forces more than a week after her unit was captured in Iraq.

TIMELINE

OCTOBER 1998

UN weapons inspectors left Iraq, Iraqi government refused to cooperate

JANUARY 2002

George W. Bush called Iraq an "axis of evil" nation in his State of the Union address

APRIL 2002

Saddam increased the reward for the families of Palestinian suicide bombers from $10,000 to $25,000

OCTOBER 2002

October 10: U.S. House voted 296-133 to grant President George W. Bush authority to remove Saddam Hussein with military force

October 11: U.S. Senate voted 77-23 to give president same power

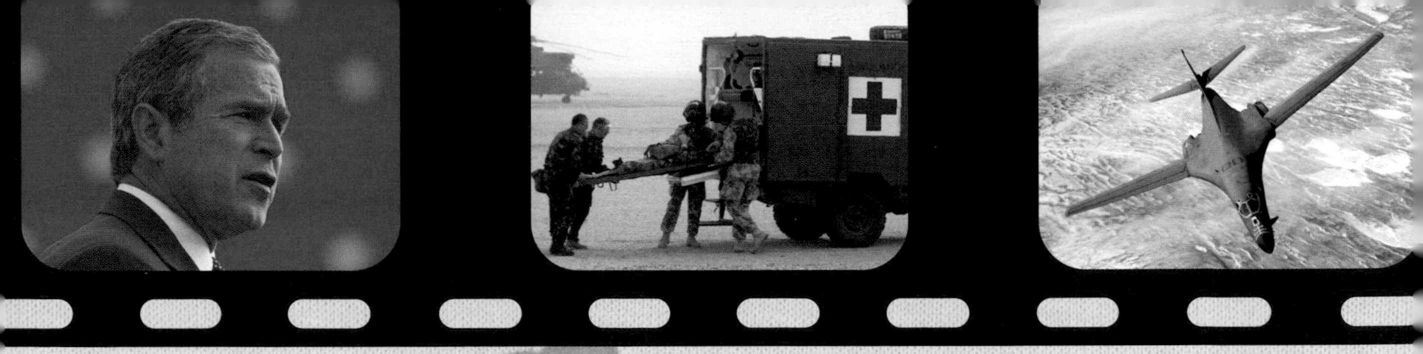

NOVEMBER 2002

November 8: UN passed Resolution 1441

November 12: Iraq rejected UN proposal

November 13: Iraq accepted UN proposal

November 18: Weapons inspectors returned to Iraq

MARCH 2003

March 17: Bush gave Saddam and sons 48 hours to leave Iraq, otherwise United States would attack

March 19: Saddam remained in Iraq, United States began attack

March 20: Iraq returned fire, coalition soldiers crossed border into Iraq

March 21: Shock and Awe campaign began

March 22: Coalition forces took control of Umm Qasr

APRIL 2003

Coalition forces reported 108 killed in the conflict, Iraqi casualties unknown

WEB SITES
WWW.ABDOPUB.COM

To learn more about the attack in Iraq, visit ABDO Publishing Company on the World Wide Web at **www.abdopub.com**. Web sites about the attack in Iraq are featured on our Book Links page. These links are routinely monitored and updated to provide the most current information available.

U.S. president George W. Bush thought a war with Iraq was necessary to remove Saddam Hussein from power.

FAST FACTS

- In January 1998, the Iraqi government stopped a weapons inspection team from entering Iraq. It felt the team had too many Americans on it. The Iraqi government said that Scott Ritter, the group's leader, was an American spy.

- Powerful Democrats such as Dick Gephardt of Missouri and Tom Daschle of South Dakota helped support the Iraq resolution. The resolution gave President Bush the power to attack Iraq if necessary. Gephardt was even one of the co-authors of the bill.

- One unit called into action during Operation Iraqi Freedom was the infantry's Third Division. This unit specialized in desert warfare.

- Iraq fired three missiles at coalition forces on March 20, 2003. At least one was a Scud missile. The UN had banned Iraq from possessing this kind of missile.

- U.S. officials were concerned that Iraqi soldiers might attempt to destroy oil wells. The destruction of these oil wells would be very damaging to the environment. During the Persian Gulf War, more than 700 Kuwaiti oil wells were destroyed. In the 2003 war, Iraqi forces were only able to destroy seven.

- To determine Saddam's true identity, a German forensic pathologist studied 450 photos of Saddam Hussein. He concluded that Saddam had three body doubles.

Glossary

Baath party:
A nonreligious political party that supports socialism and is committed to uniting all Arabs against Western influence.

casualty:
A military person lost through death, wounds, injury, sickness, or capture, or listed as missing in action. A civilian casualty is a nonmilitary person killed or injured during war.

Central Intelligence Agency (CIA):
An agency of the U.S. government that evaluates global threats to national security.

convoy:
A large group of individual units traveling together for protection.

Fedayeen Saddam:
A paramilitary group that supported Saddam Hussein.

forensic:
A science used to evaluate and find facts in court cases.

Global Positioning System (GPS):
Satellite signals, run through a receiver, that tell the inner computer the time, position, and velocity of the weapon.

paramilitary group:
A force formed using a military pattern, and sometimes used as an auxiliary military force.

pathologist:
A physician who studies diseases and how they are caused.

Persian Gulf War:
The war fought between the United States and its allies against Iraq in 1991. The war began after Iraq invaded its neighbor, Kuwait.

regime:
A government in power.

Republican Guard:
Saddam Hussein's best-trained troops.

State of the Union address:
The U.S. president's annual speech that summarizes the condition of the nation.

Taliban:
An Islamic fundamentalist government that once ruled Afghanistan.

United Nations (UN):
A group of nations formed in 1945. Its goals are peace, human rights, security, and social and economic development.

weapons of mass destruction (WMD):
Weapons that kill or injure large numbers of people, or cause massive damage to buildings. When people talk about weapons of mass destruction, they are usually referring to nuclear, biological, or chemical weapons.

INDEX